GRAPHIC LIBRARY™

INVENTIONS AND DISCOVERY

LEVI STRAUSS AND BLUE JEANS

by Nathan Olson

illustrated by Dave Hoover, Keith Williams,
and Charles Barnett III

Consultant:
John Mark Lambertson
Director and Archivist
National Frontier Trails Museum
Independence, Missouri

Capstone press

Mankato, Minnesota

Graphic Library is published by Capstone Press,
1710 Roe Crest Drive, North Mankato, Minnesota 56003.
www.capstonepub.com

Library of Congress Cataloging-in-Publication Data
Olson, Nathan.
    Levi Strauss and blue jeans / by Nathan Olson ; illustrated by Dave Hoover, Keith Williams,
and Charles Barnett III.
    p. cm.—(Graphic library. Inventions and discovery)
    Includes bibliographical references and index.
    ISBN-13: 978-0-7368-6484-8 (hardcover)   ISBN-10: 0-7368-6484-9 (hardcover)
    ISBN-13: 978-0-7368-9646-7 (softcover pbk.)   ISBN-10: 0-7368-9646-5 (softcover pbk.)
    1. Strauss, Levi, 1829–1902—Juvenile literature. 2. Levi Strauss and Company—History
—Juvenile literature. 3. Jeans (Clothing)—California—History—Juvenile literature. 4. Jeans
(Clothing)—California—History—Comic books, strips, etc. I. Hoover, Dave, 1955– II. Williams,
Keith, 1958 Feb. 24– III. Barnett, Charles, III. IV. Title. V. Series.
HD9940.U4S7974 2007
338.7'687113092—dc22   2006008310

Summary: In graphic novel format, tells the story of Levi Strauss and the evolution of blue jeans.

Art Direction and Design
Bob Lentz

Colorist
Matt Webb

Editor
Donald Lemke

Printed in the United States of America in North Mankato, Minnesota.
102015
009312R

TABLE OF CONTENTS

CHAPTER 1
Gold Fever 4

CHAPTER 2
Reaching California 10

CHAPTER 3
Those Pants of Levi's 16

CHAPTER 4
Big Business. 22

More about Strauss and Blue Jeans 28
Glossary 30
Internet Sites 30
Read More 31
Bibliography 31
Index 32

Chapter 1
Gold Fever

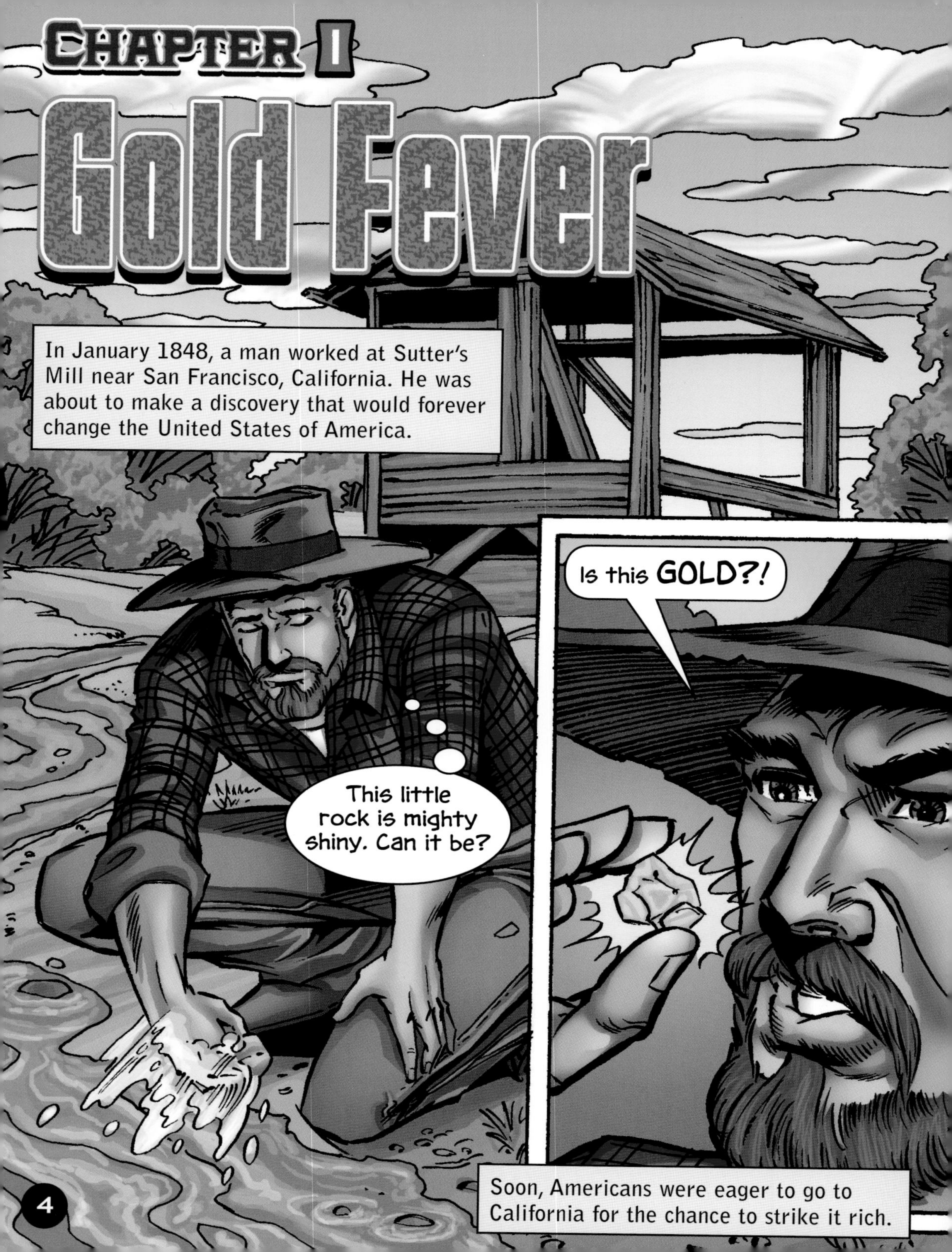
In January 1848, a man worked at Sutter's Mill near San Francisco, California. He was about to make a discovery that would forever change the United States of America.
This little rock is mighty shiny. Can it be?
Is this GOLD?!
Soon, Americans were eager to go to California for the chance to strike it rich.

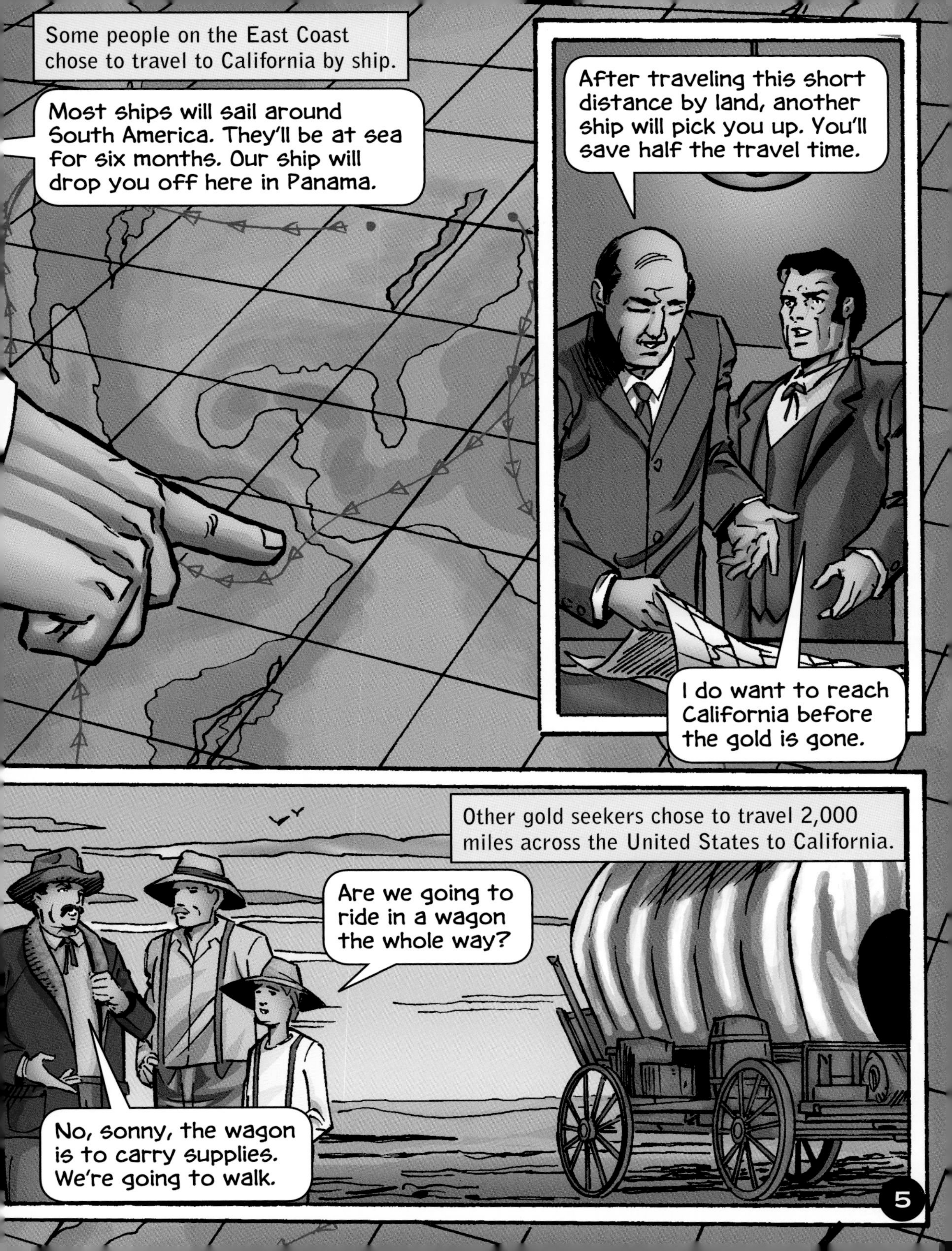

Some people on the East Coast chose to travel to California by ship.
Most ships will sail around South America. They'll be at sea for six months. Our ship will drop you off here in Panama.
After traveling this short distance by land, another ship will pick you up. You'll save half the travel time.
I do want to reach California before the gold is gone.
Other gold seekers chose to travel 2,000 miles across the United States to California.
Are we going to ride in a wagon the whole way?
No, sonny, the wagon is to carry supplies. We're going to walk.

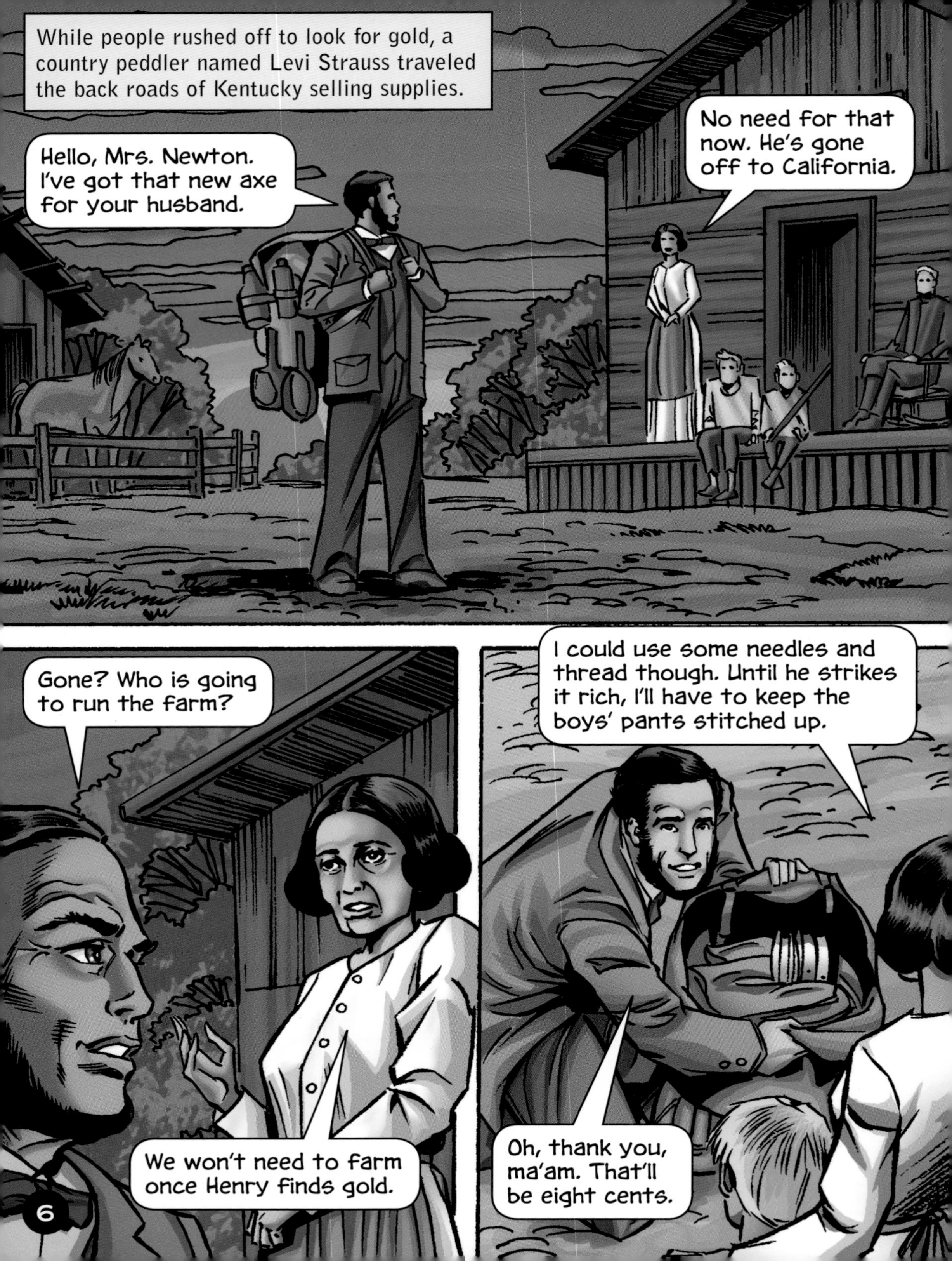
While people rushed off to look for gold, a country peddler named Levi Strauss traveled the back roads of Kentucky selling supplies.
Hello, Mrs. Newton. I've got that new axe for your husband.
No need for that now. He's gone off to California.
Gone? Who is going to run the farm?
We won't need to farm once Henry finds gold.
I could use some needles and thread though. Until he strikes it rich, I'll have to keep the boys' pants stitched up.
Oh, thank you, ma'am. That'll be eight cents.

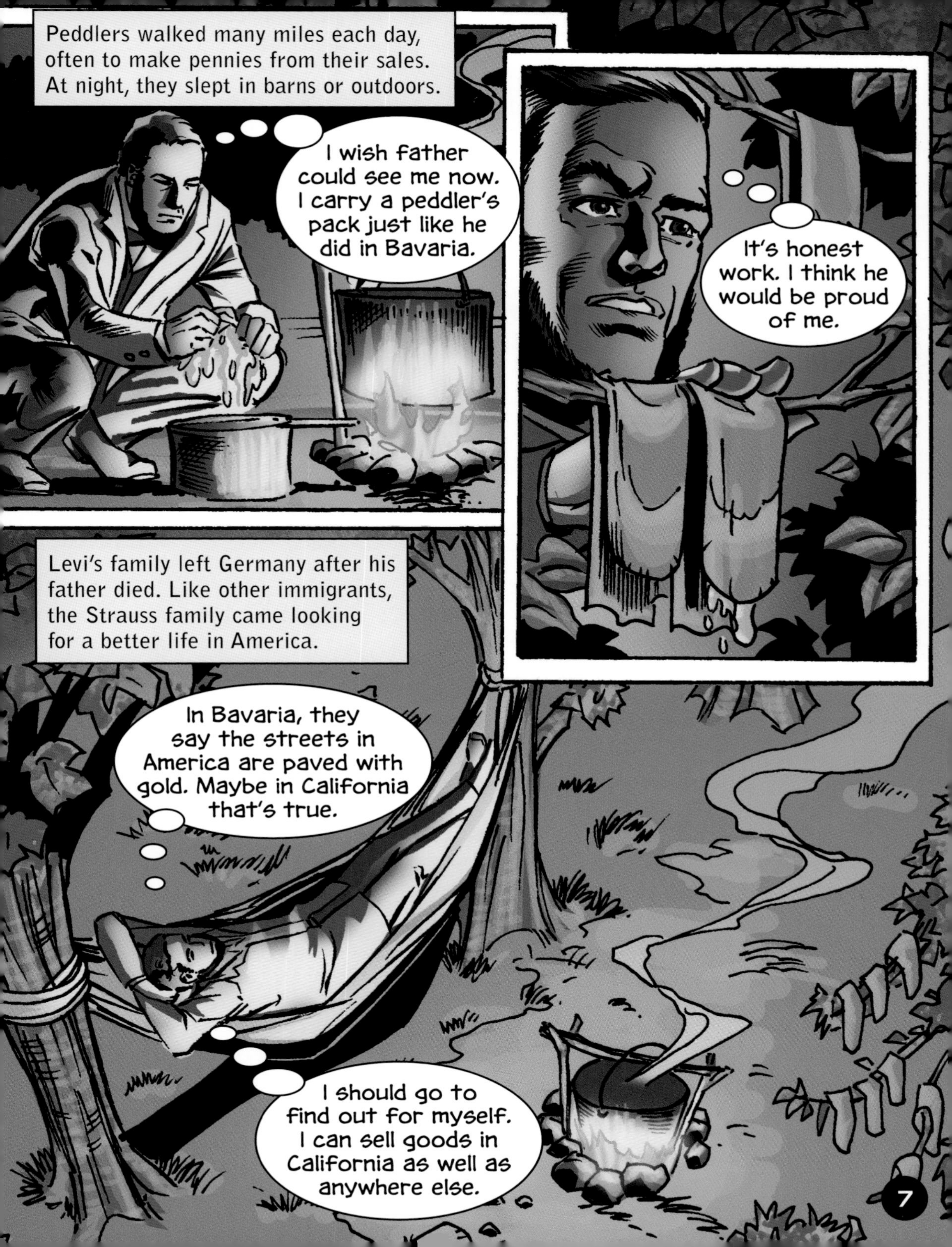

Peddlers walked many miles each day, often to make pennies from their sales. At night, they slept in barns or outdoors.
I wish father could see me now. I carry a peddler's pack just like he did in Bavaria.
It's honest work. I think he would be proud of me.
Levi's family left Germany after his father died. Like other immigrants, the Strauss family came looking for a better life in America.
In Bavaria, they say the streets in America are paved with gold. Maybe in California that's true.
I should go to find out for myself. I can sell goods in California as well as anywhere else.

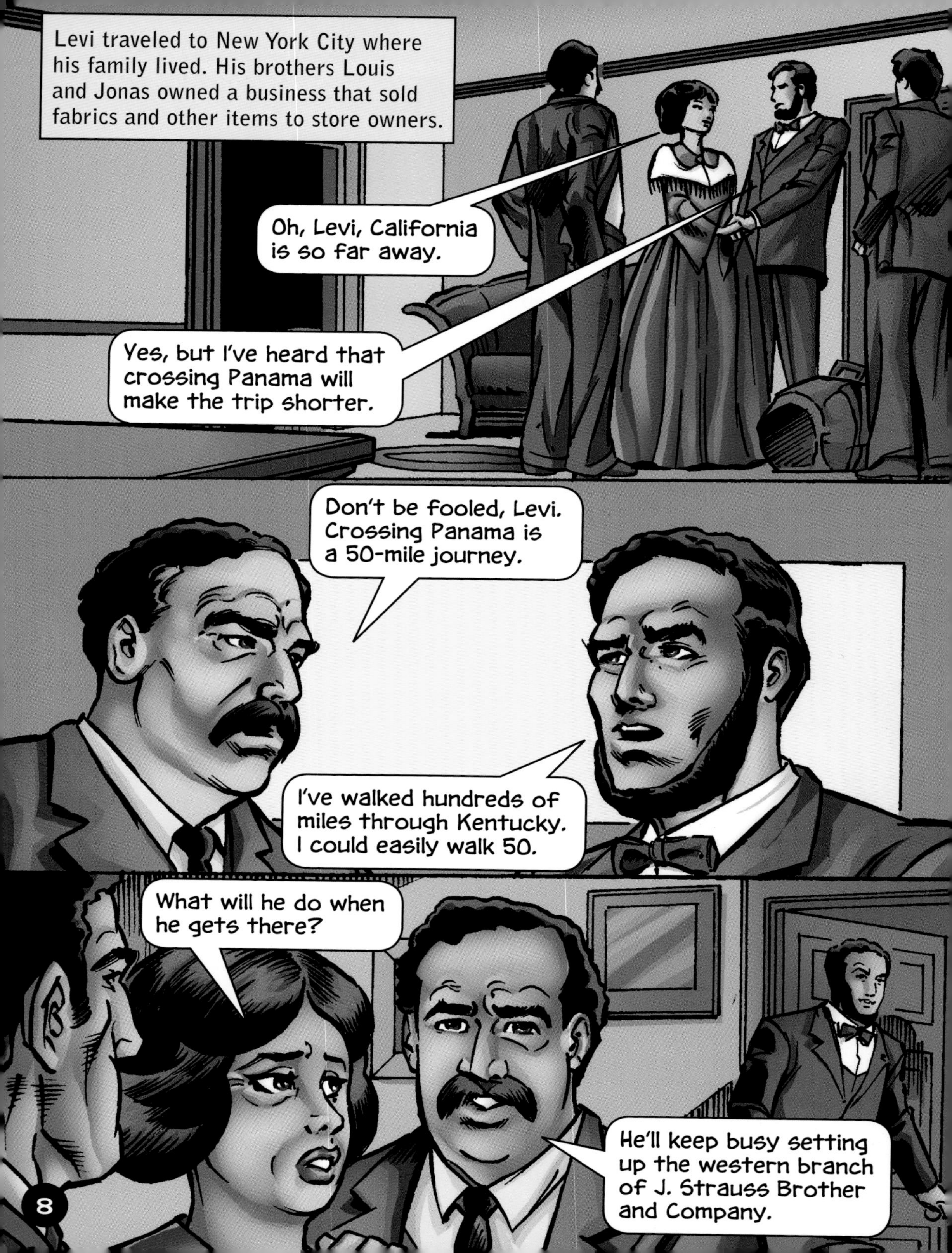
Levi traveled to New York City where his family lived. His brothers Louis and Jonas owned a business that sold fabrics and other items to store owners.
Oh, Levi, California is so far away.
Yes, but I've heard that crossing Panama will make the trip shorter.
Don't be fooled, Levi. Crossing Panama is a 50-mile journey.
I've walked hundreds of miles through Kentucky. I could easily walk 50.
What will he do when he gets there?
He'll keep busy setting up the western branch of J. Strauss Brother and Company.

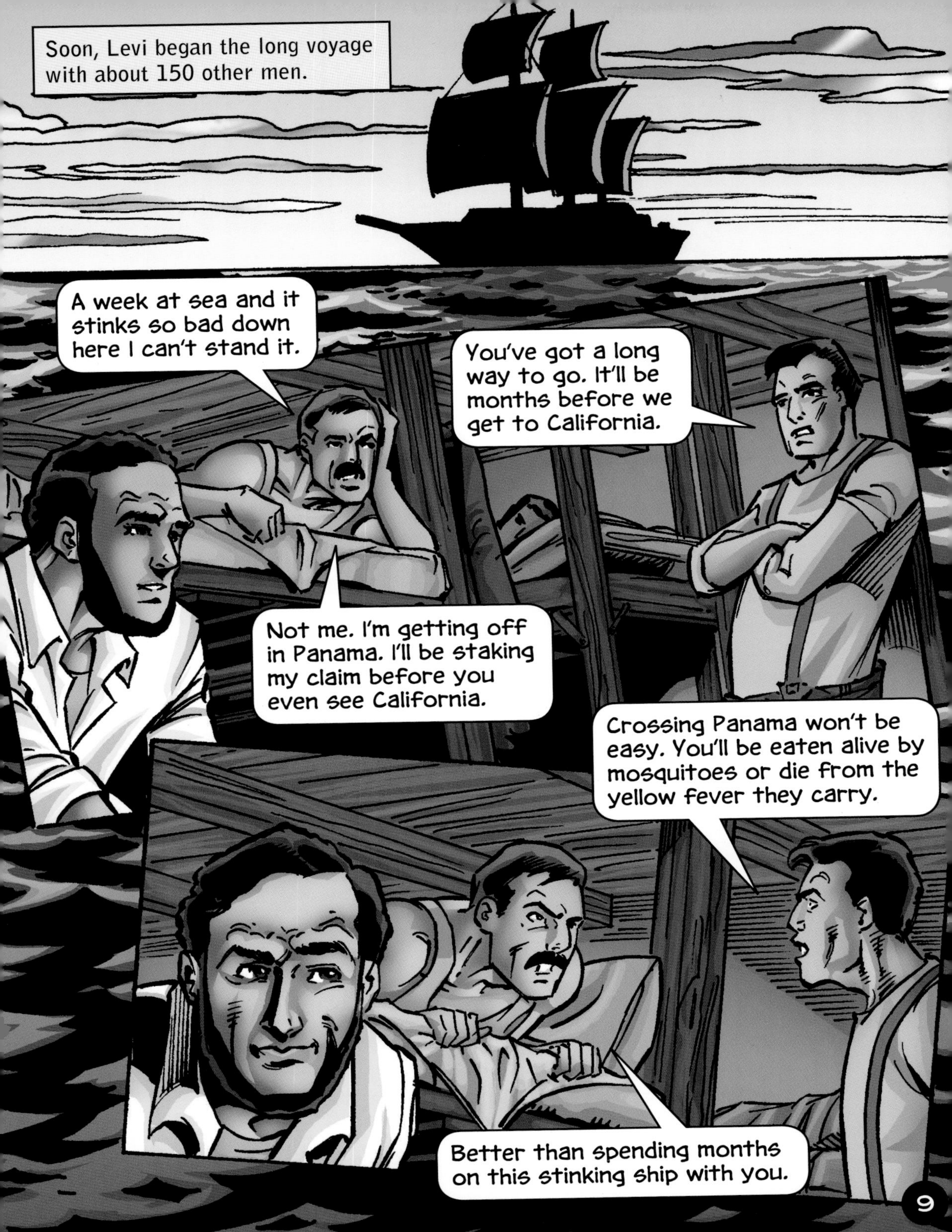
Soon, Levi began the long voyage with about 150 other men.
A week at sea and it stinks so bad down here I can't stand it.
You've got a long way to go. It'll be months before we get to California.
Not me. I'm getting off in Panama. I'll be staking my claim before you even see California.
Crossing Panama won't be easy. You'll be eaten alive by mosquitoes or die from the yellow fever they carry.
Better than spending months on this stinking ship with you.

CHAPTER 2

Reaching California

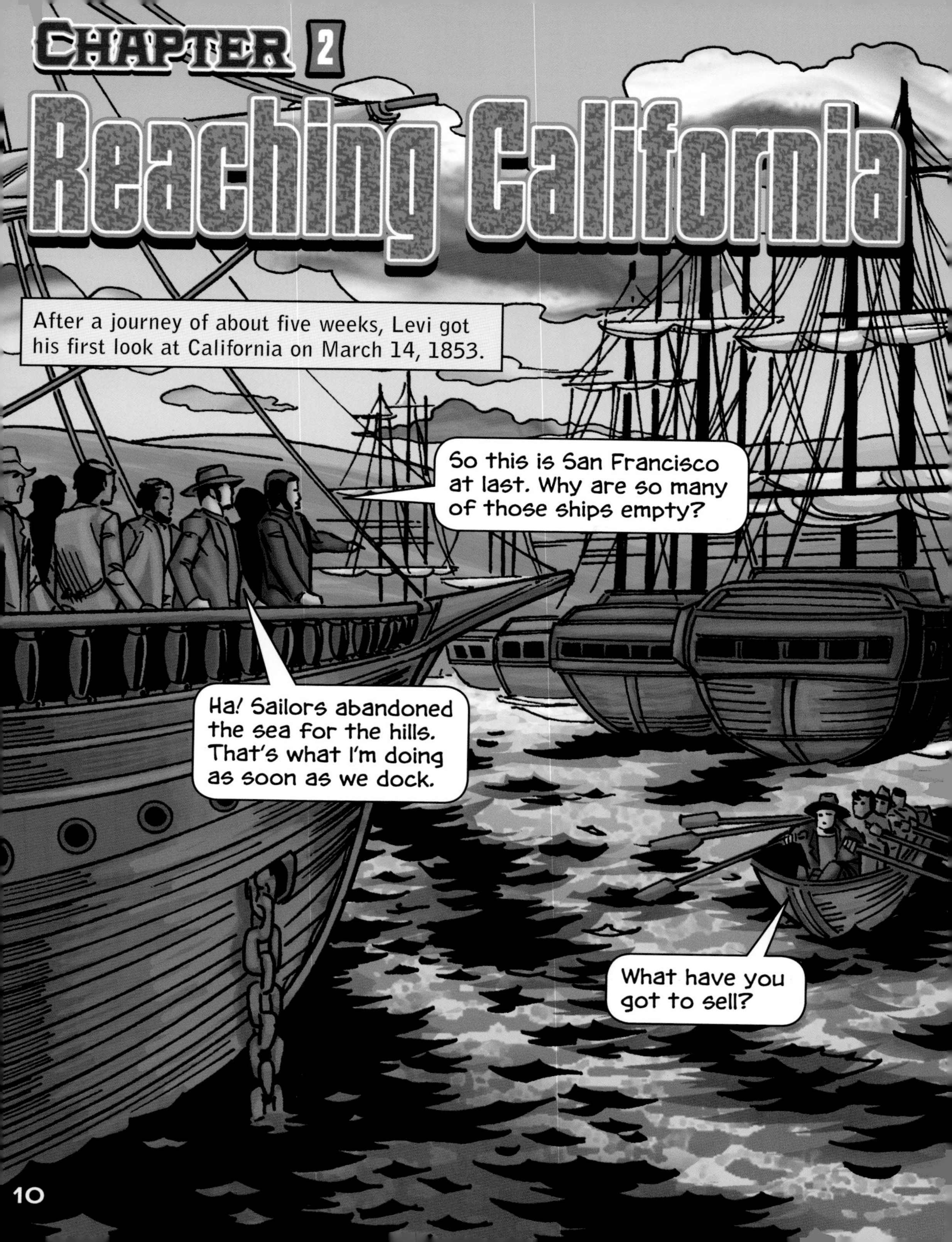

After a journey of about five weeks, Levi got his first look at California on March 14, 1853.
So this is San Francisco at last. Why are so many of those ships empty?
Ha! Sailors abandoned the sea for the hills. That's what I'm doing as soon as we dock.
What have you got to sell?

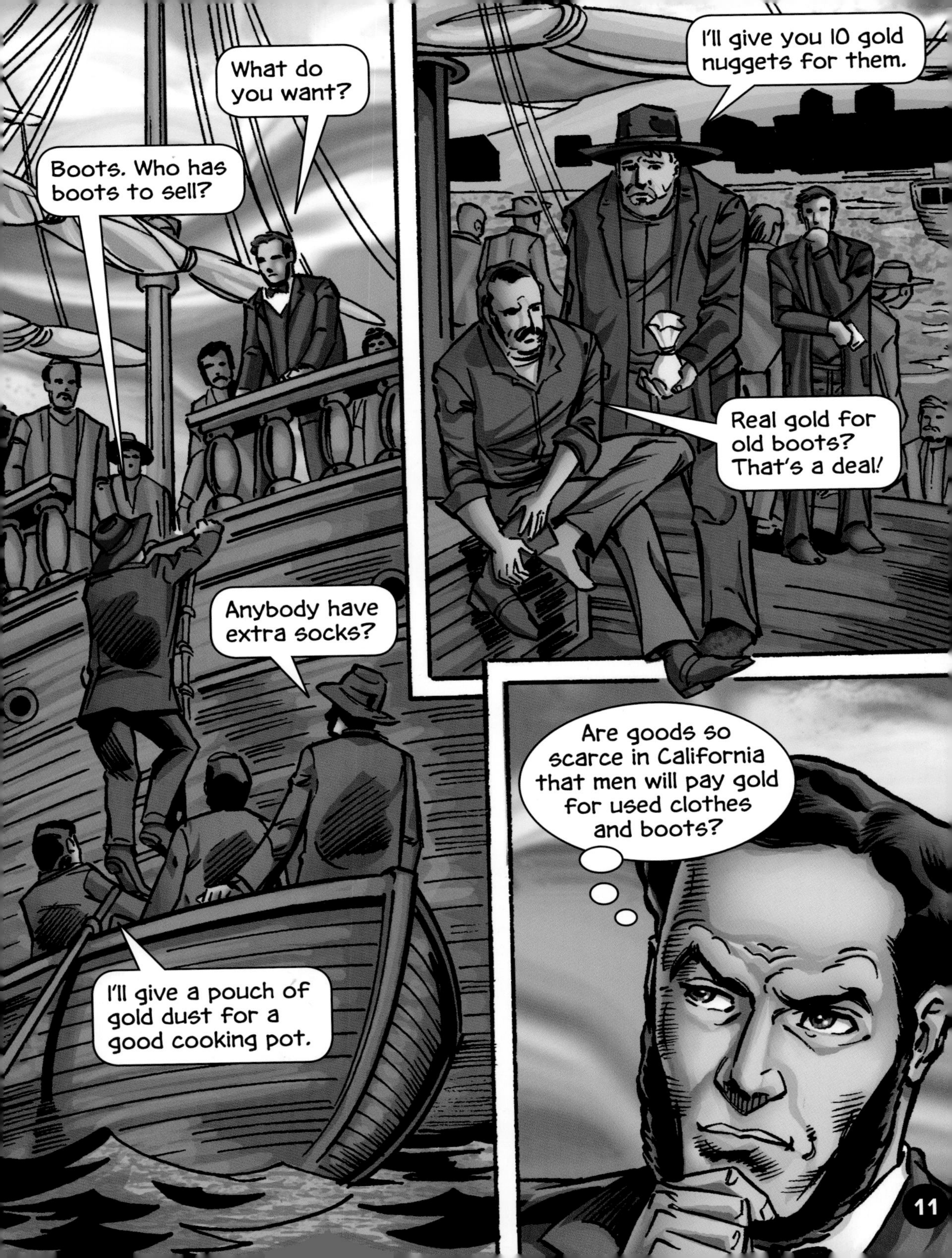

Boots. Who has boots to sell?
What do you want?
I'll give you 10 gold nuggets for them.
Real gold for old boots? That's a deal!
Anybody have extra socks?
I'll give a pouch of gold dust for a good cooking pot.
Are goods so scarce in California that men will pay gold for used clothes and boots?

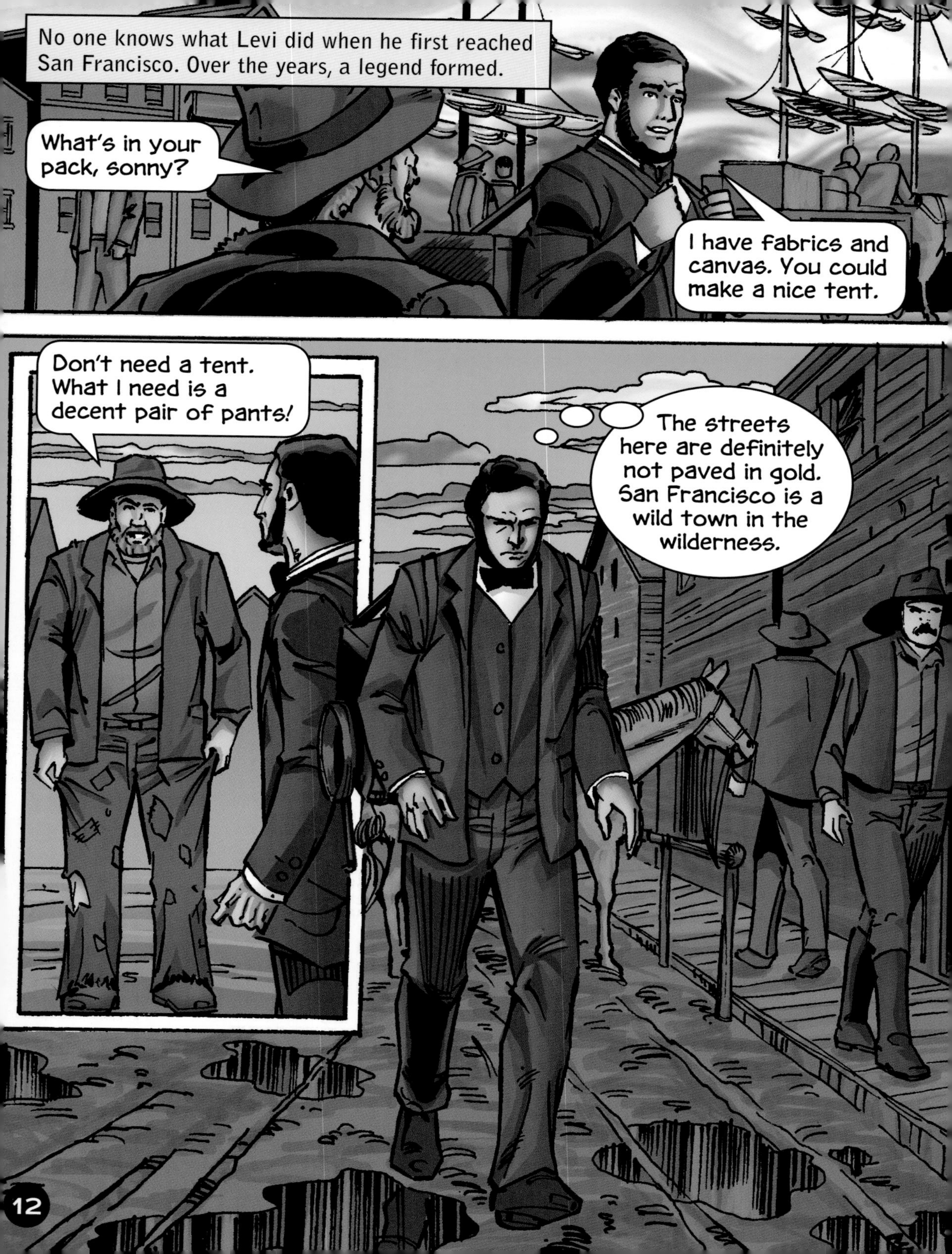
No one knows what Levi did when he first reached San Francisco. Over the years, a legend formed.
What's in your pack, sonny?
I have fabrics and canvas. You could make a nice tent.
Don't need a tent. What I need is a decent pair of pants!
The streets here are definitely not paved in gold. San Francisco is a wild town in the wilderness.

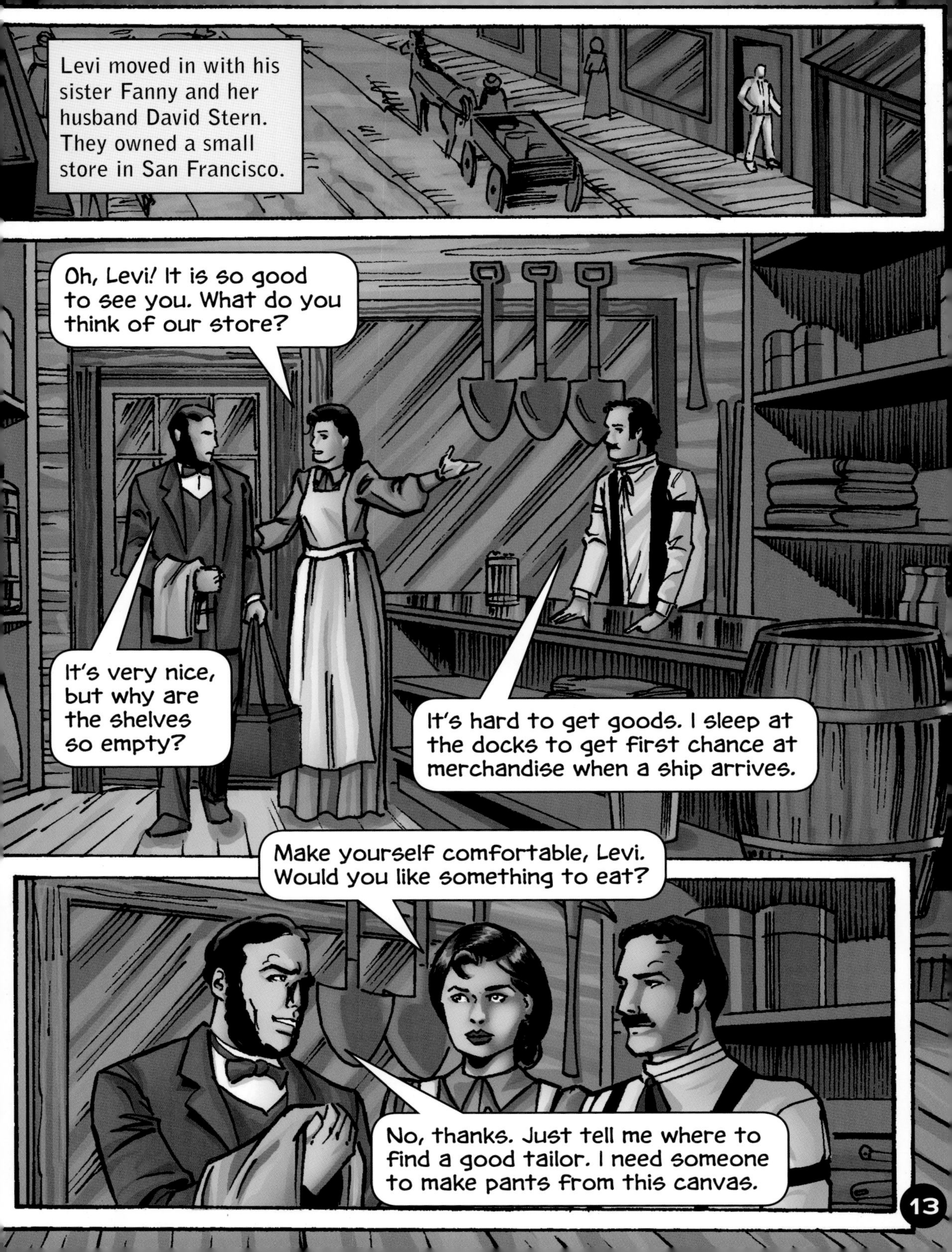
Levi moved in with his sister Fanny and her husband David Stern. They owned a small store in San Francisco.
Oh, Levi! It is so good to see you. What do you think of our store?
It's very nice, but why are the shelves so empty?
It's hard to get goods. I sleep at the docks to get first chance at merchandise when a ship arrives.
Make yourself comfortable, Levi. Would you like something to eat?
No, thanks. Just tell me where to find a good tailor. I need someone to make pants from this canvas.

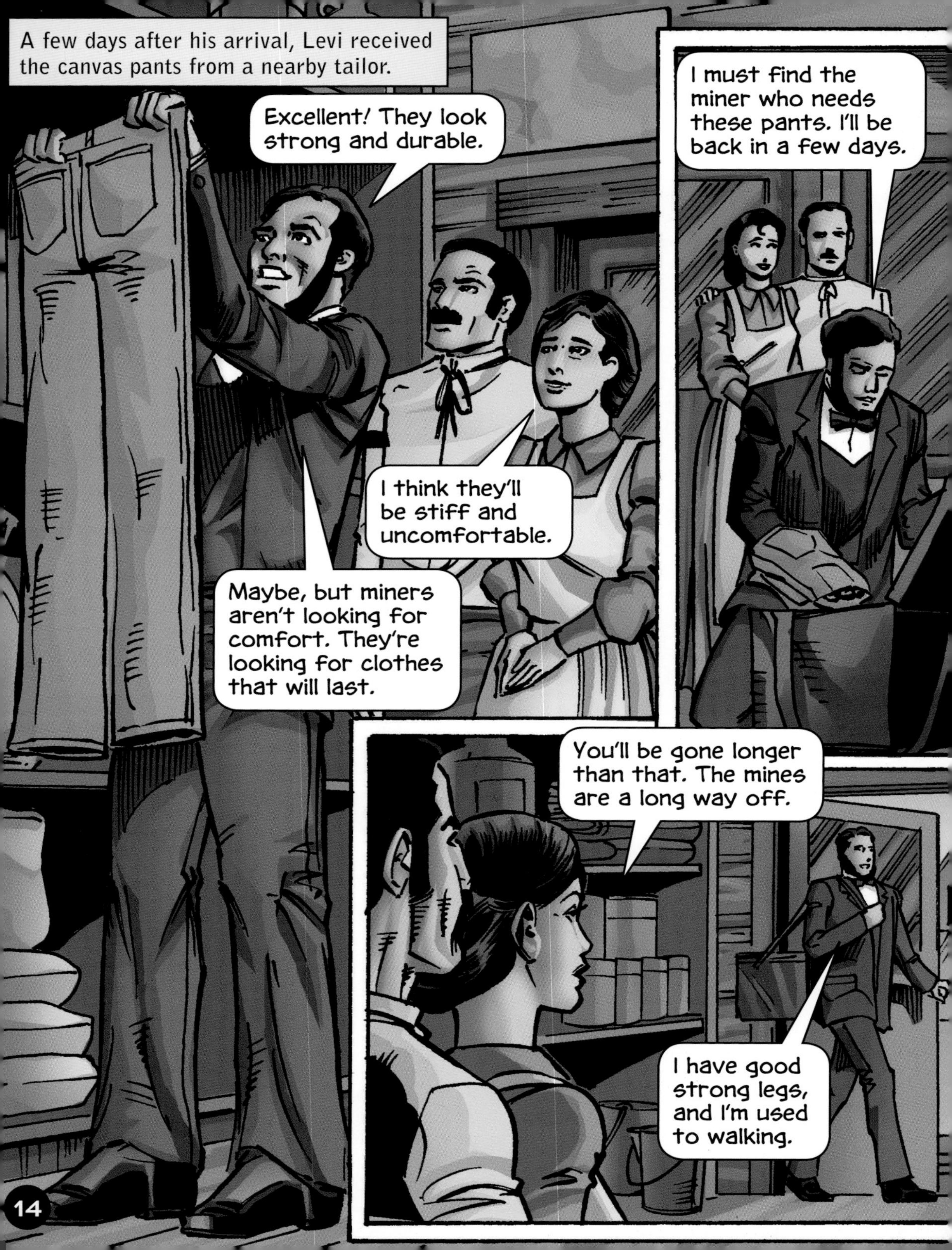
A few days after his arrival, Levi received the canvas pants from a nearby tailor.
Excellent! They look strong and durable.
I think they'll be stiff and uncomfortable.
Maybe, but miners aren't looking for comfort. They're looking for clothes that will last.
I must find the miner who needs these pants. I'll be back in a few days.
You'll be gone longer than that. The mines are a long way off.
I have good strong legs, and I'm used to walking.

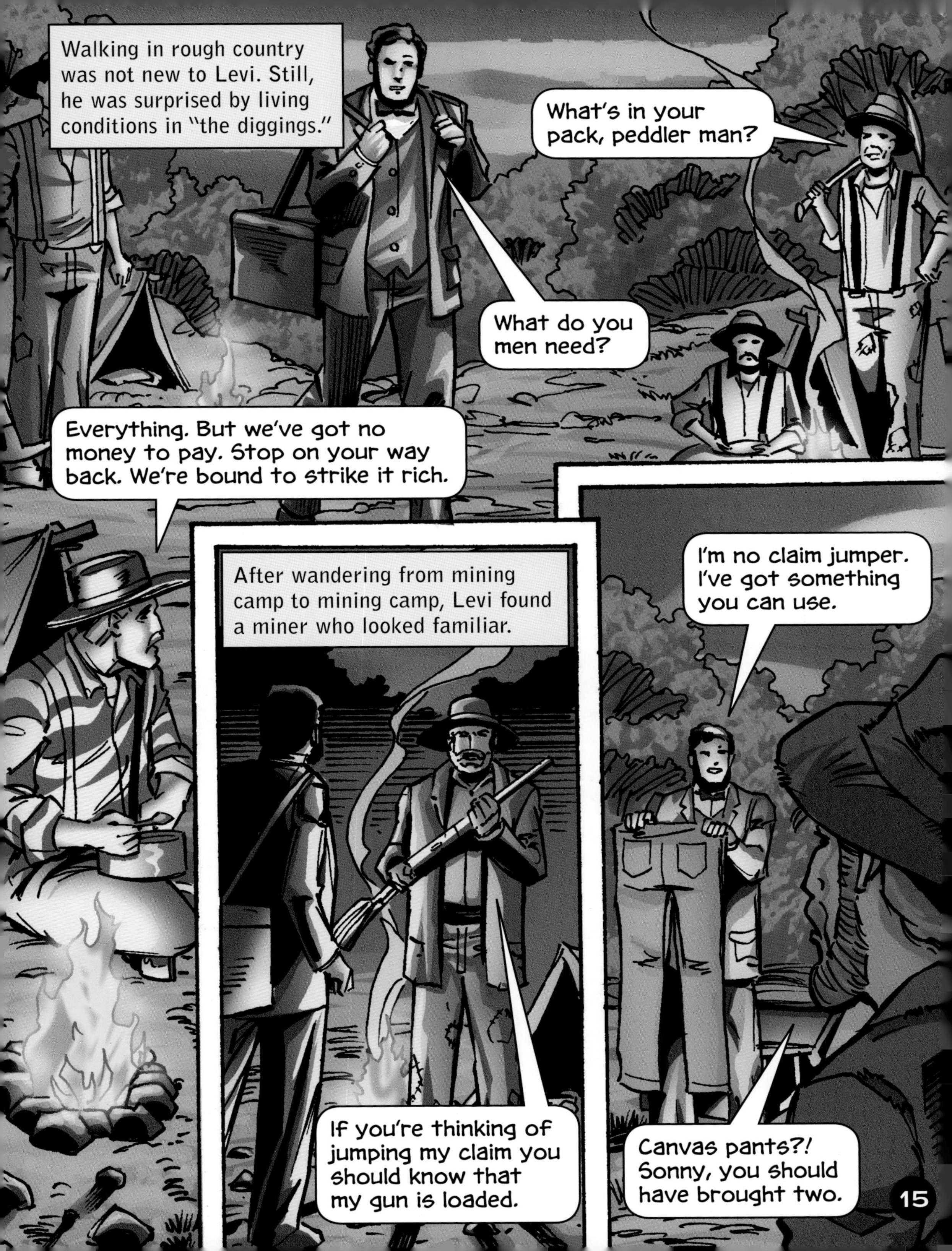
Walking in rough country was not new to Levi. Still, he was surprised by living conditions in "the diggings."
What's in your pack, peddler man?
What do you men need?
Everything. But we've got no money to pay. Stop on your way back. We're bound to strike it rich.
After wandering from mining camp to mining camp, Levi found a miner who looked familiar.
If you're thinking of jumping my claim you should know that my gun is loaded.
I'm no claim jumper. I've got something you can use.
Canvas pants?! Sonny, you should have brought two.

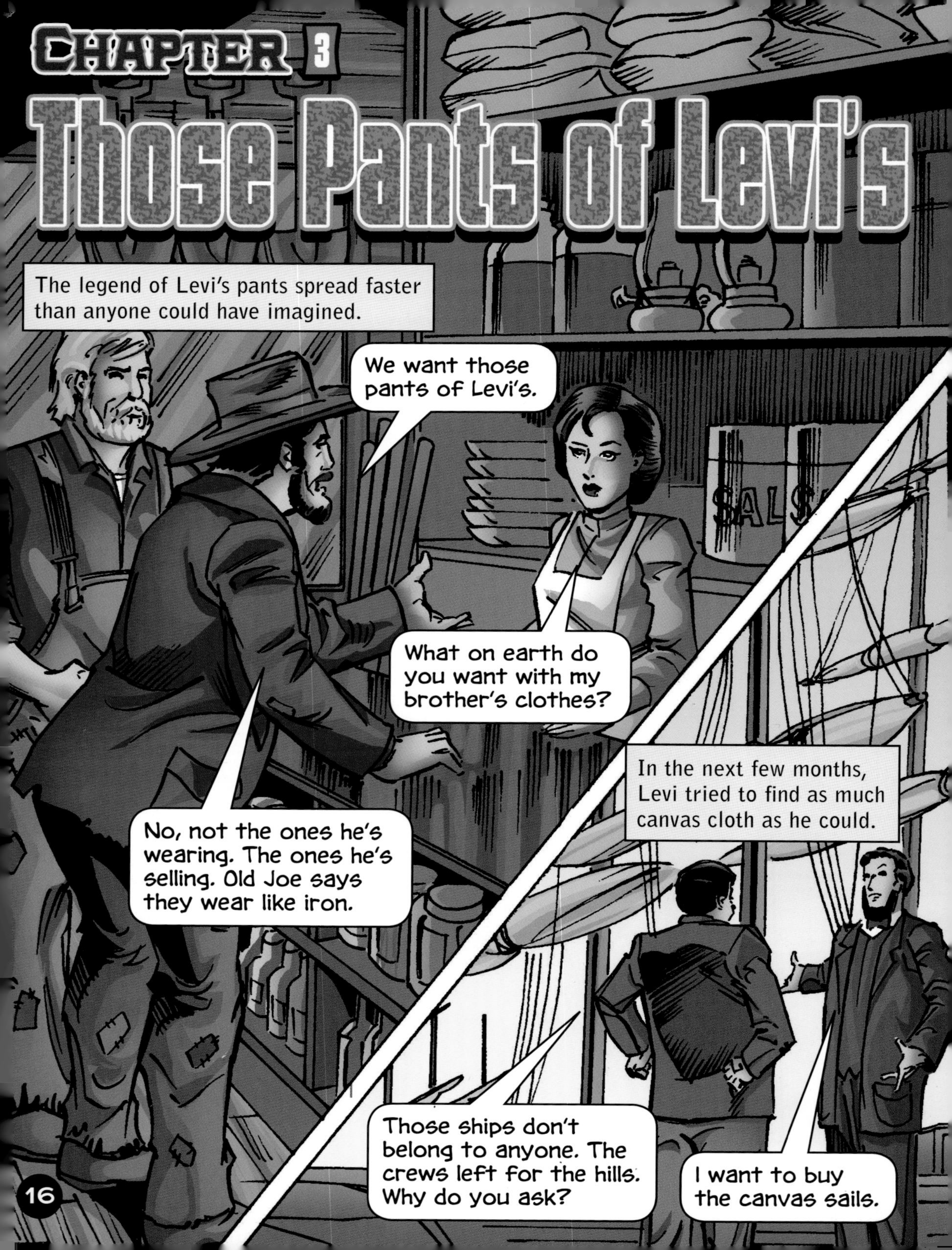

CHAPTER 3
Those Pants of Levi's
The legend of Levi's pants spread faster than anyone could have imagined.
We want those pants of Levi's.
What on earth do you want with my brother's clothes?
No, not the ones he's wearing. The ones he's selling. Old Joe says they wear like iron.
In the next few months, Levi tried to find as much canvas cloth as he could.
I want to buy the canvas sails.
Those ships don't belong to anyone. The crews left for the hills. Why do you ask?

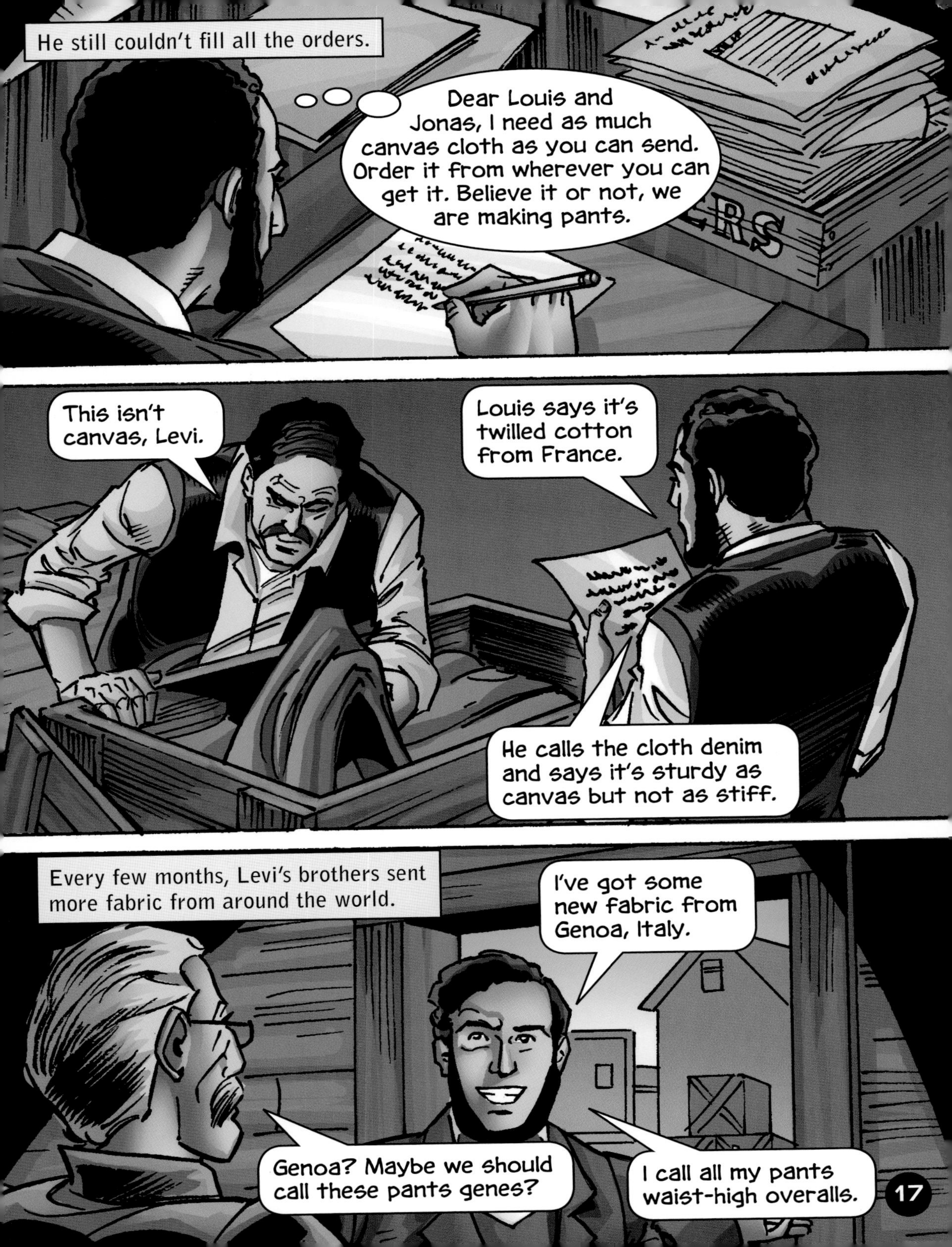
He still couldn't fill all the orders.
Dear Louis and Jonas, I need as much canvas cloth as you can send. Order it from wherever you can get it. Believe it or not, we are making pants.
This isn't canvas, Levi.
Louis says it's twilled cotton from France.
He calls the cloth denim and says it's sturdy as canvas but not as stiff.
Every few months, Levi's brothers sent more fabric from around the world.
I've got some new fabric from Genoa, Italy.
Genoa? Maybe we should call these pants genes?
I call all my pants waist-high overalls.

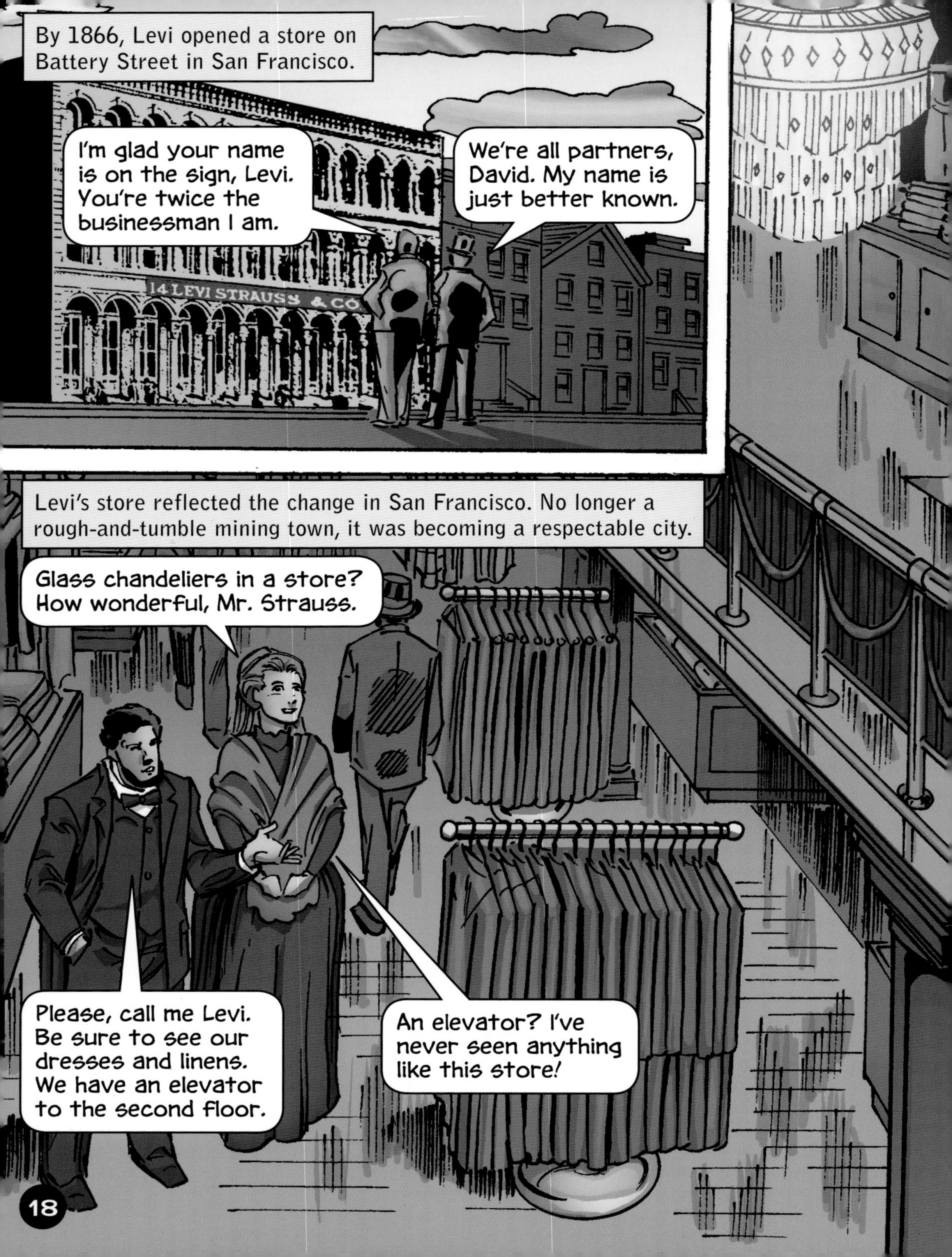
By 1866, Levi opened a store on Battery Street in San Francisco.
I'm glad your name is on the sign, Levi. You're twice the businessman I am.
We're all partners, David. My name is just better known.
14 LEVI STRAUSS & CO.
Levi's store reflected the change in San Francisco. No longer a rough-and-tumble mining town, it was becoming a respectable city.
Glass chandeliers in a store? How wonderful, Mr. Strauss.
Please, call me Levi. Be sure to see our dresses and linens. We have an elevator to the second floor.
An elevator? I've never seen anything like this store!

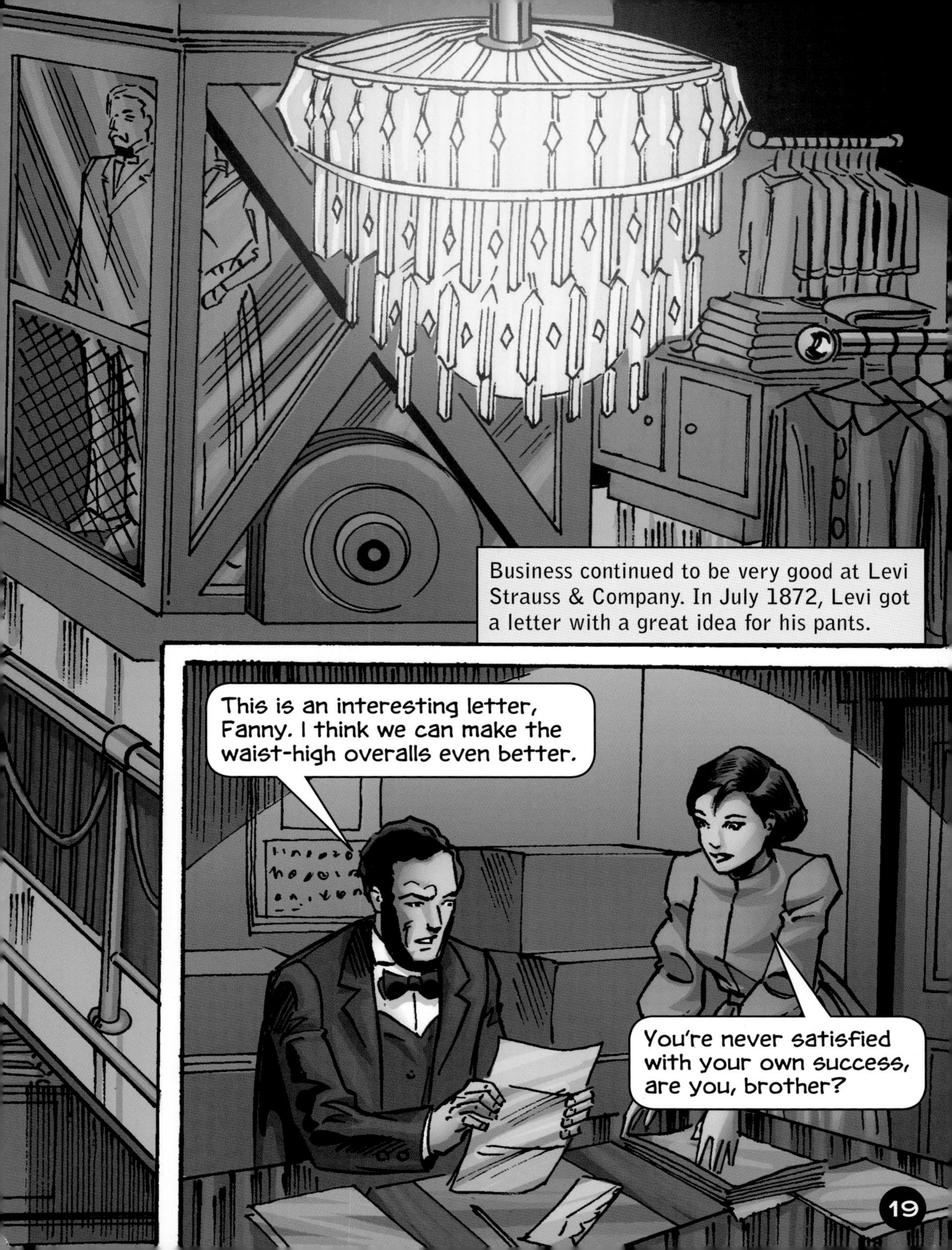
Business continued to be very good at Levi Strauss & Company. In July 1872, Levi got a letter with a great idea for his pants.
This is an interesting letter, Fanny. I think we can make the waist-high overalls even better.
You're never satisfied with your own success, are you, brother?

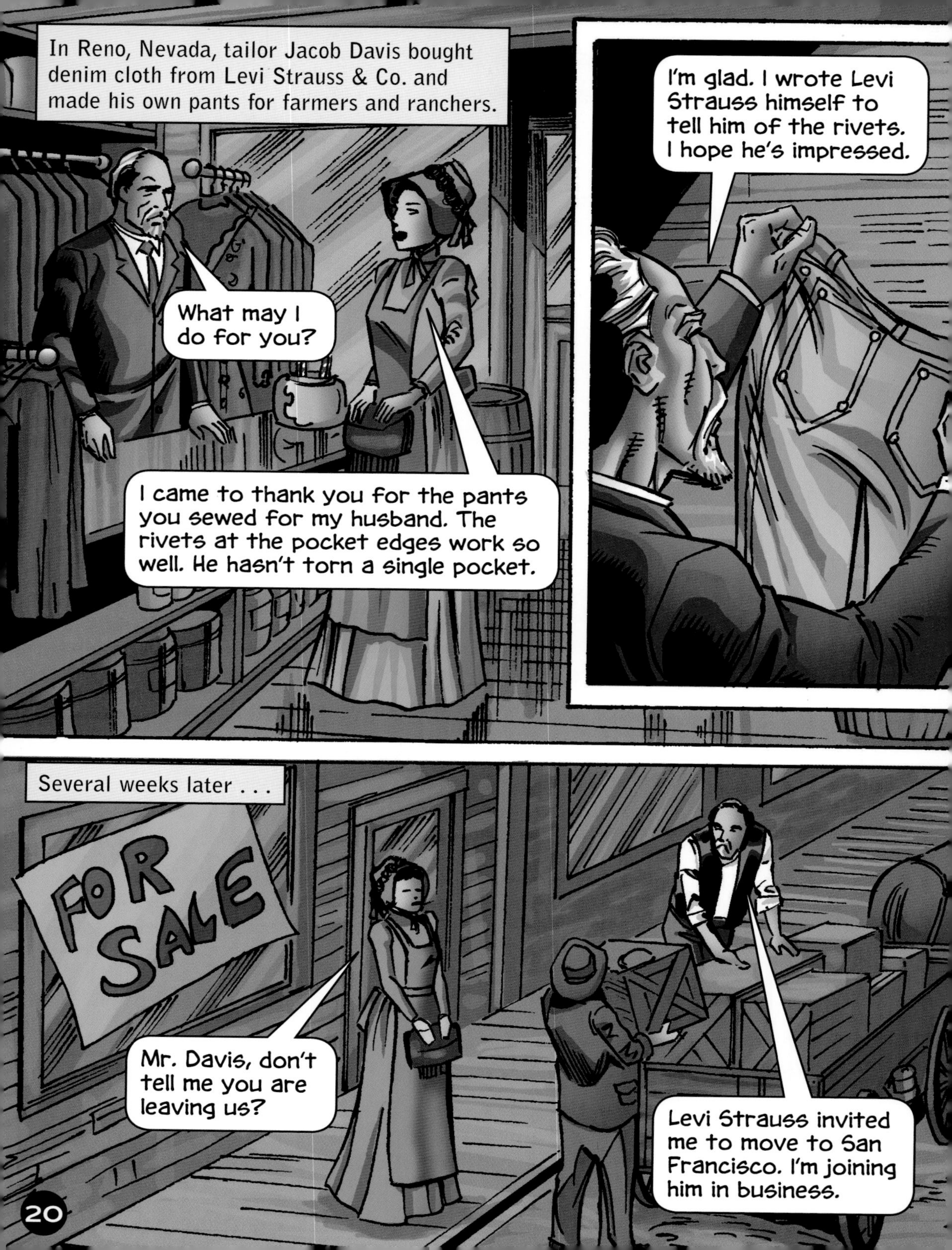

In Reno, Nevada, tailor Jacob Davis bought denim cloth from Levi Strauss & Co. and made his own pants for farmers and ranchers.
What may I do for you?
I came to thank you for the pants you sewed for my husband. The rivets at the pocket edges work so well. He hasn't torn a single pocket.
I'm glad. I wrote Levi Strauss himself to tell him of the rivets. I hope he's impressed.
Several weeks later . . .
FOR SALE
Mr. Davis, don't tell me you are leaving us?
Levi Strauss invited me to move to San Francisco. I'm joining him in business.

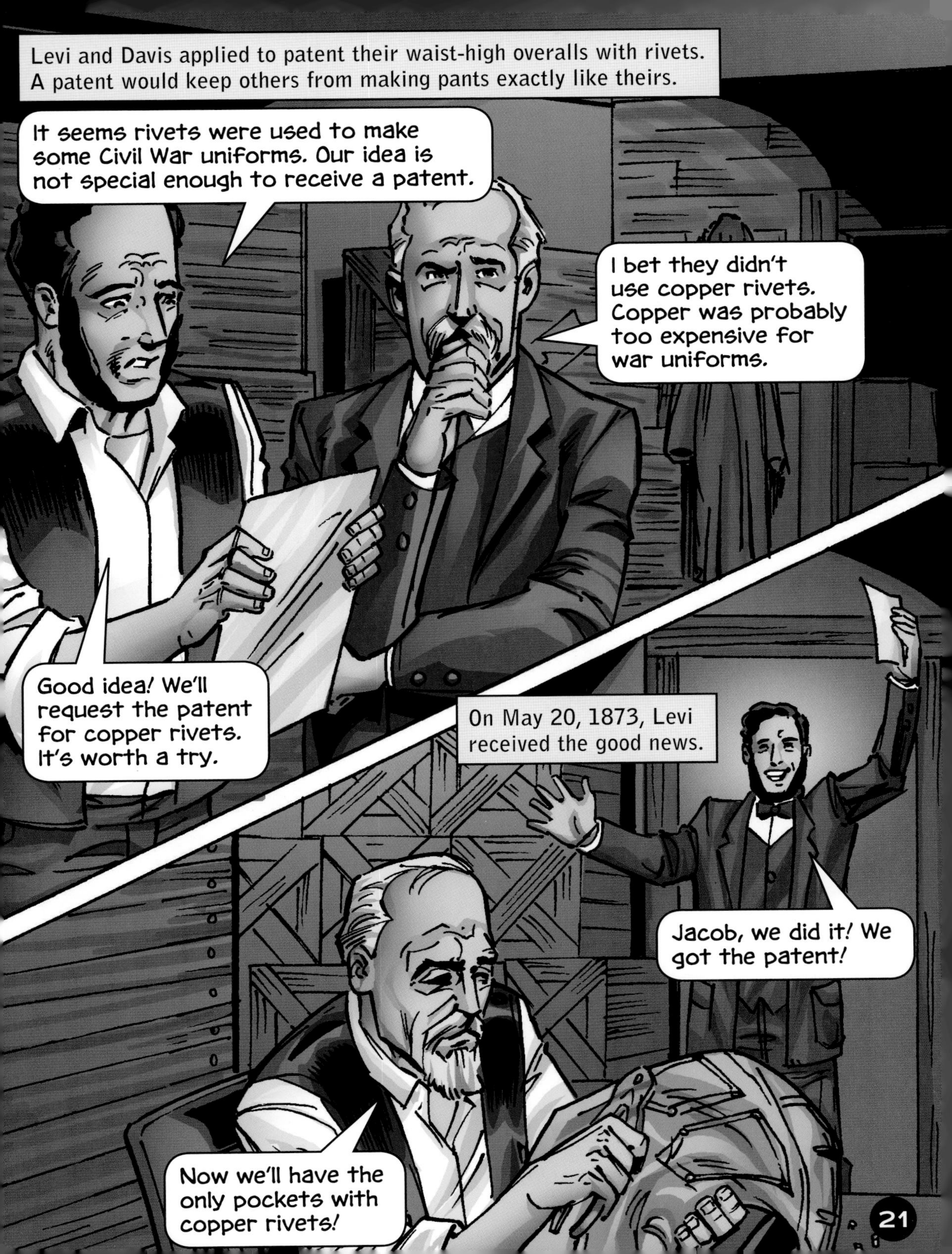
Levi and Davis applied to patent their waist-high overalls with rivets. A patent would keep others from making pants exactly like theirs.
It seems rivets were used to make some Civil War uniforms. Our idea is not special enough to receive a patent.
I bet they didn't use copper rivets. Copper was probably too expensive for war uniforms.
Good idea! We'll request the patent for copper rivets. It's worth a try.
On May 20, 1873, Levi received the good news.
Jacob, we did it! We got the patent!
Now we'll have the only pockets with copper rivets!

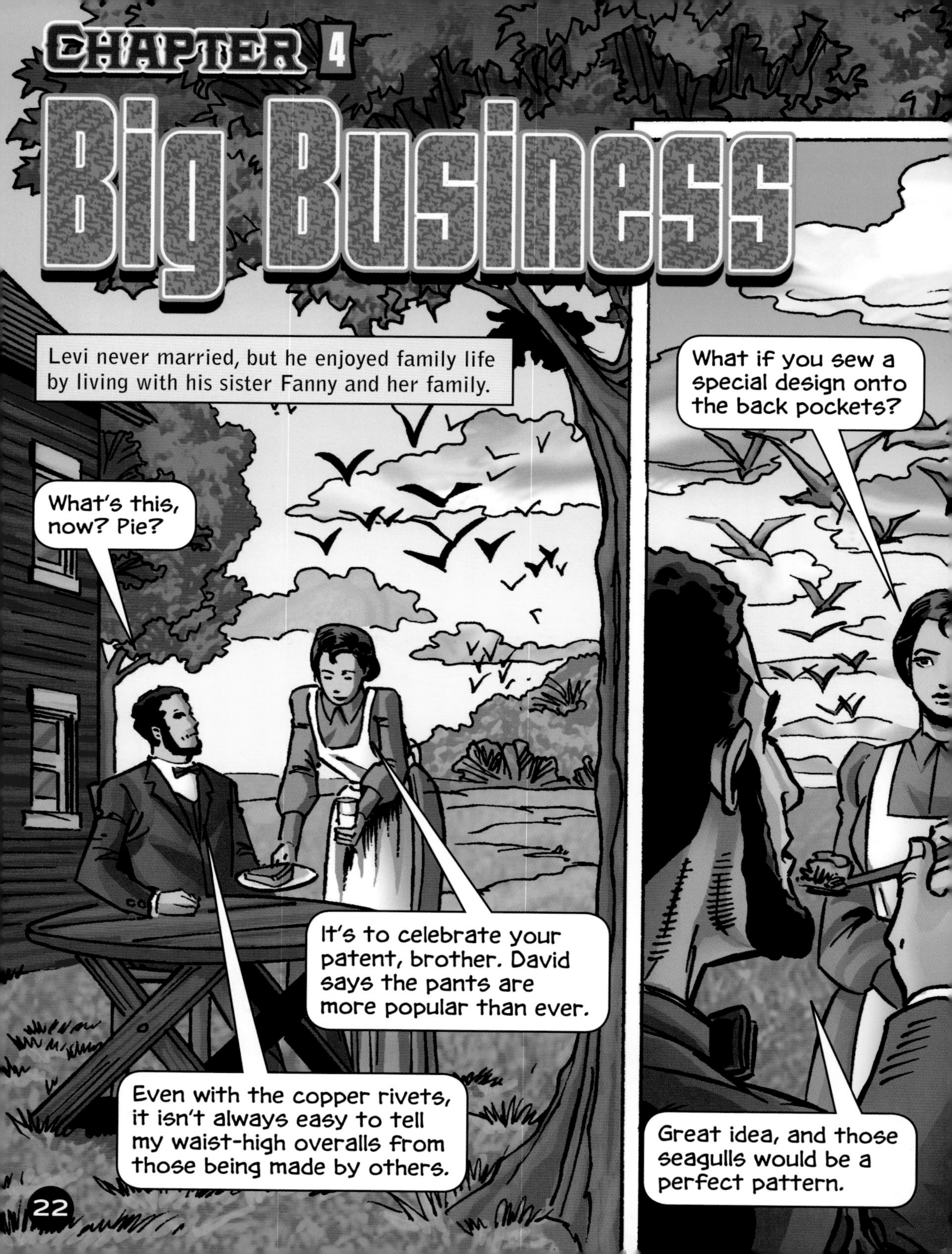
CHAPTER 4
Big Business
Levi never married, but he enjoyed family life by living with his sister Fanny and her family.
What's this, now? Pie?
It's to celebrate your patent, brother. David says the pants are more popular than ever.
Even with the copper rivets, it isn't always easy to tell my waist-high overalls from those being made by others.
What if you sew a special design onto the back pockets?
Great idea, and those seagulls would be a perfect pattern.

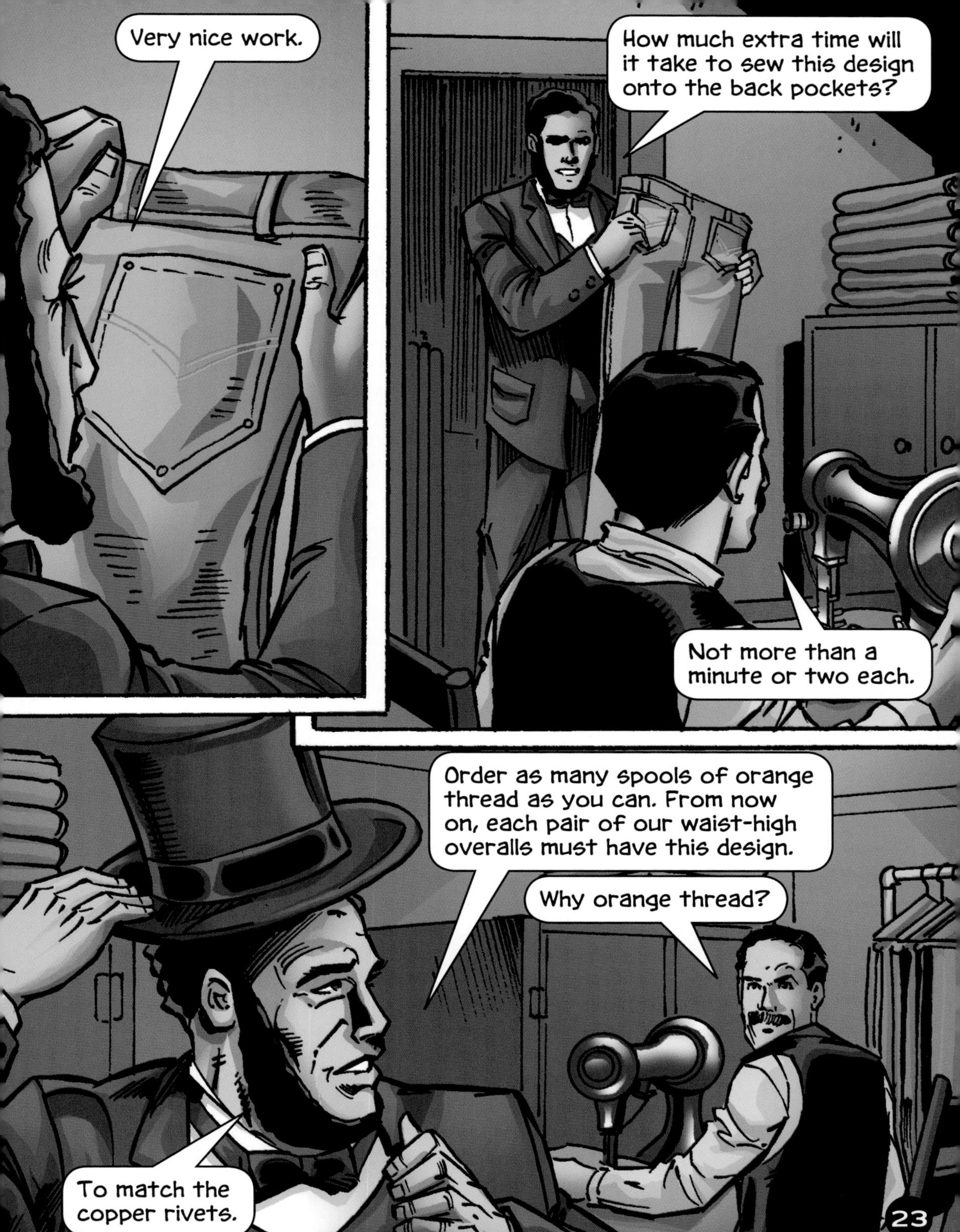
Very nice work.
How much extra time will it take to sew this design onto the back pockets?
Not more than a minute or two each.
Order as many spools of orange thread as you can. From now on, each pair of our waist-high overalls must have this design.
Why orange thread?
To match the copper rivets.

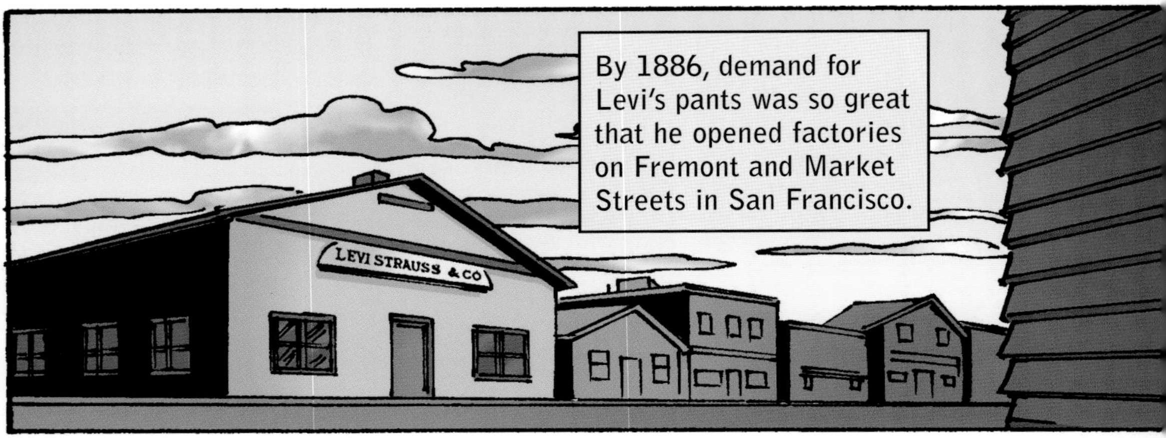
By 1886, demand for Levi's pants was so great that he opened factories on Fremont and Market Streets in San Francisco.
LEVI STRAUSS & CO

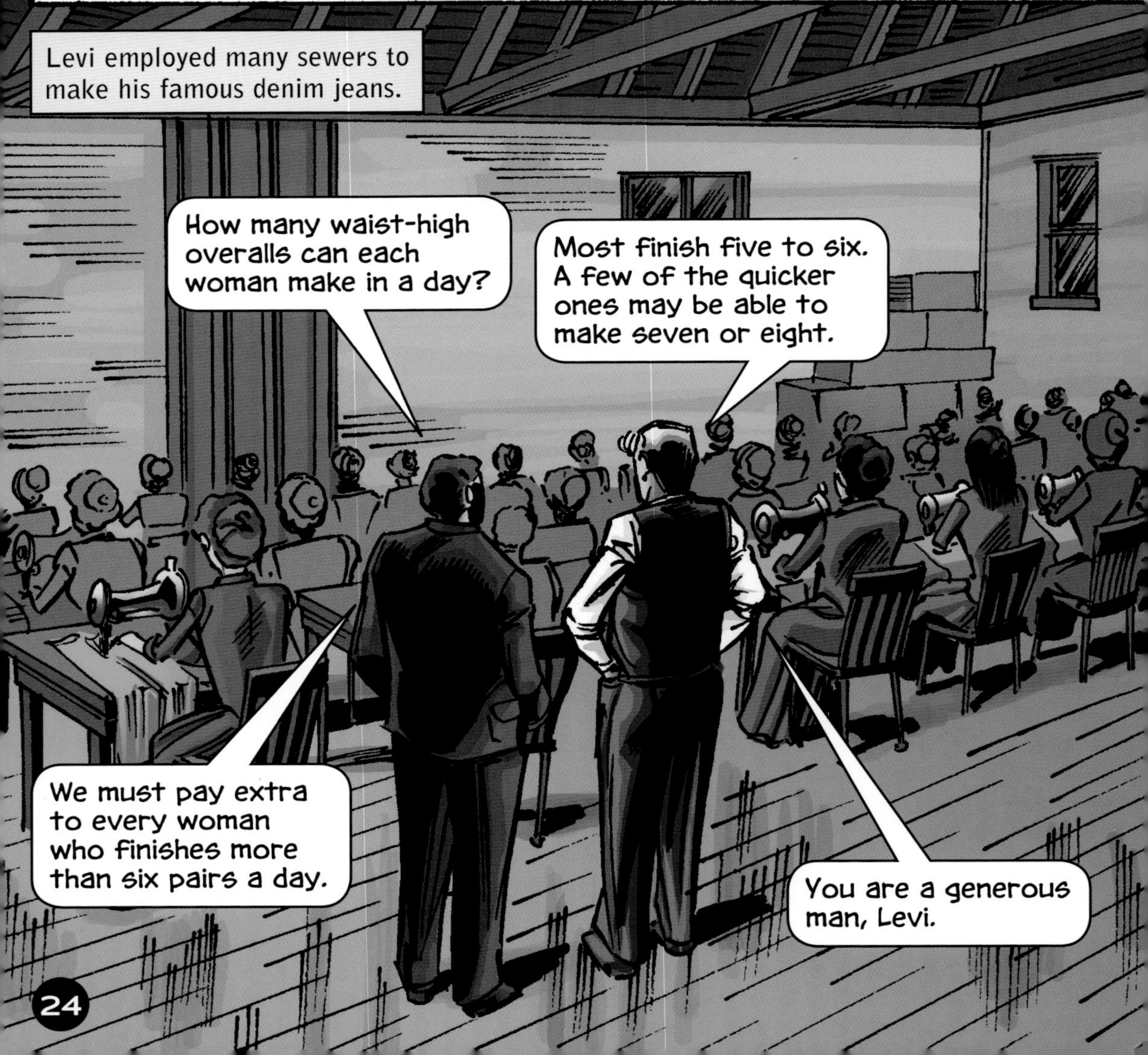
Levi employed many sewers to make his famous denim jeans.
How many waist-high overalls can each woman make in a day?
Most finish five to six. A few of the quicker ones may be able to make seven or eight.
We must pay extra to every woman who finishes more than six pairs a day.
You are a generous man, Levi.

Levi's success in business made him a notable man in San Francisco.

Hello, Mr. Strauss.

Please, call me Levi.

Tell me, Levi, why a successful man like you has never married.

Oh, but I am. You see, I am married to my business. And now, please forgive me. I must hurry over to my factory.

Look, Jacob, these leather patches will advertise how sturdy and durable our waist-high overalls are.

Leather patches? Wherever will we put them?

LEVI STRAUSS & CO.
SAN FRANCISCO
ORIGINAL RIVETED
QUALITY CLOTHING
TRADE MARK

On the waistband of every pair we make.

Let me guess. We stitch these on with orange thread, right?

The style of pants that carried this new leather emblem was called 501. Levi's 501 jeans are still sold today.

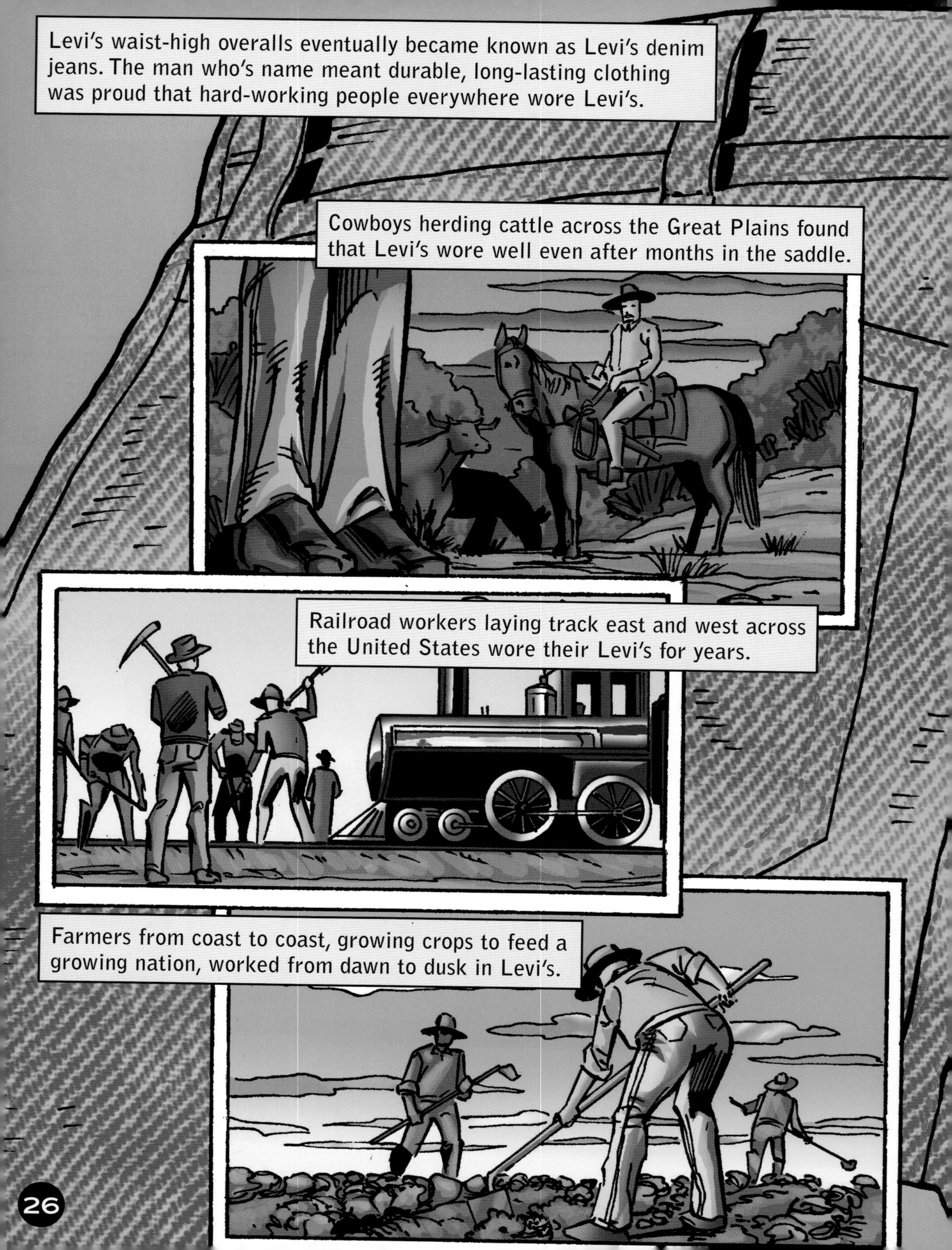
Levi's waist-high overalls eventually became known as Levi's denim jeans. The man who's name meant durable, long-lasting clothing was proud that hard-working people everywhere wore Levi's.
Cowboys herding cattle across the Great Plains found that Levi's wore well even after months in the saddle.
Railroad workers laying track east and west across the United States wore their Levi's for years.
Farmers from coast to coast, growing crops to feed a growing nation, worked from dawn to dusk in Levi's.

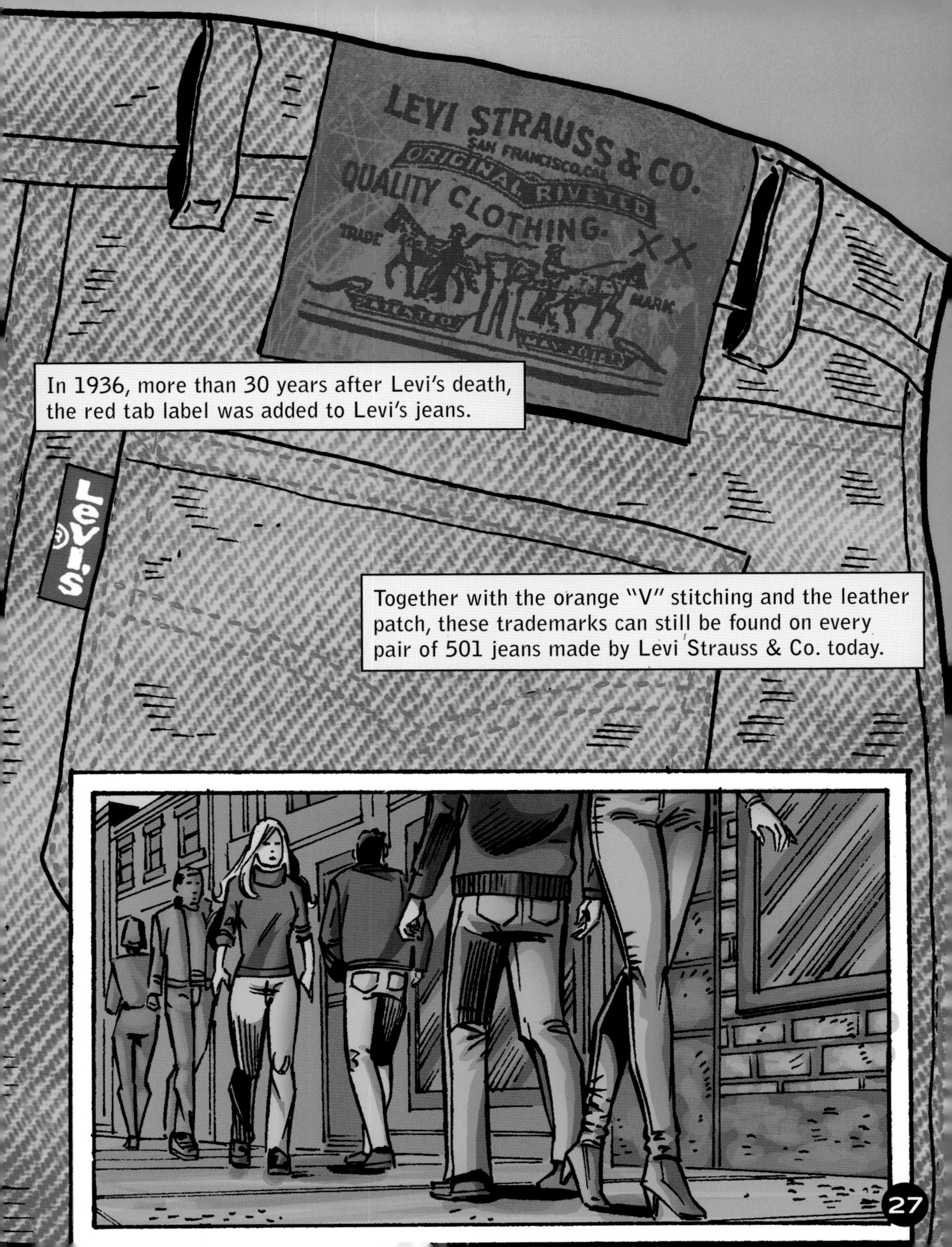
LEVI STRAUSS & CO.
SAN FRANCISCO, CAL.
ORIGINAL RIVETED
QUALITY CLOTHING.
TRADE MARK
XX
In 1936, more than 30 years after Levi's death, the red tab label was added to Levi's jeans.
Levi's
Together with the orange "V" stitching and the leather patch, these trademarks can still be found on every pair of 501 jeans made by Levi Strauss & Co. today.

MORE ABOUT STRAUSS
AND BLUE JEANS

Levi's In 1906, a great earthquake struck San Francisco, igniting fires that destroyed much of the city. Historical records for Levi Strauss & Co. were destroyed. Many details about the life of Levi Strauss are based on legends rather than historical facts. Historians believe the story of Strauss making canvas pants for a gold miner is a myth. Such a legend probably grew from the need for sturdy clothing and the popularity of denim pants with pocket rivets.

Levi's Levi Strauss was born Loeb Strauss in Buttenheim, Bavaria, on February 26, 1829. He moved to New York in 1847, and by 1850 he was known as Levi Strauss. At the age of 73, Strauss died on September 26, 1902, in San Francisco, California.

Levi's Levi's father, Hirsch Strauss, was a dry goods peddler in Bavaria. His four children with his first wife were Jacob, Jonas, Lippman (later called Louis), and Maila (later called Mary). After his first wife died in 1822, Hirsch married Rebecca Haas. They had two children, Vogela (later called Fanny) and Loeb (later called Levi).

Levi's A typical pair of Levi's 501 jeans takes almost 2 yards of denim, 213 yards of thread, five buttons, and six rivets.

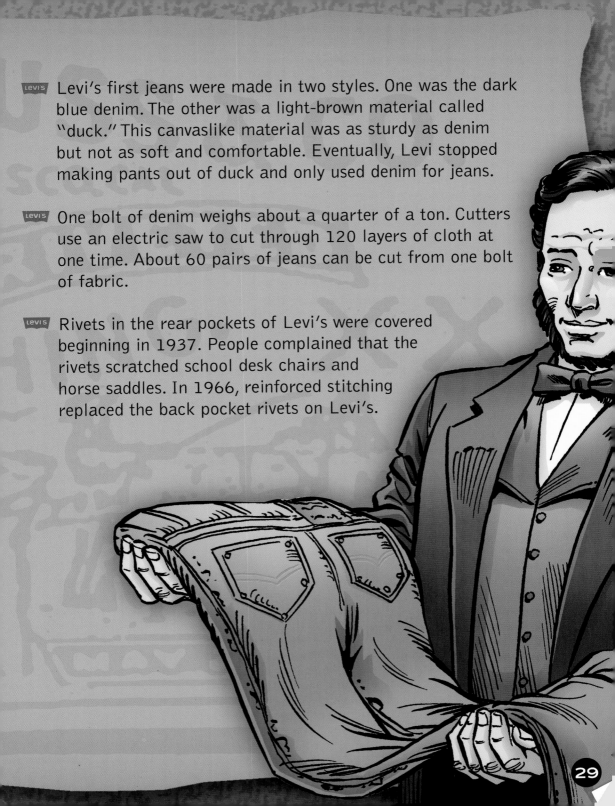

Levi's first jeans were made in two styles. One was the dark blue denim. The other was a light-brown material called "duck." This canvaslike material was as sturdy as denim but not as soft and comfortable. Eventually, Levi stopped making pants out of duck and only used denim for jeans.

One bolt of denim weighs about a quarter of a ton. Cutters use an electric saw to cut through 120 layers of cloth at one time. About 60 pairs of jeans can be cut from one bolt of fabric.

Rivets in the rear pockets of Levi's were covered beginning in 1937. People complained that the rivets scratched school desk chairs and horse saddles. In 1966, reinforced stitching replaced the back pocket rivets on Levi's.

GLOSSARY

canvas (KAN-vuhss)—a type of coarse, strong cloth used for tents, sails, and clothing

denim (DEN-im)—strong cotton material used to make jeans and other articles of clothing

patent (PAT-uhnt)—a legal document giving someone sole rights to manufacture or sell a product

rivet (RIV-it)—a strong metal bolt that is used to fasten something together

trademark (TRADE-mark)—a symbol that shows that a product is made by a particular company

INTERNET SITES

FactHound offers a safe, fun way to find Internet sites related to this book. All of the sites on FactHound have been researched by our staff.

Here's how:
1. Visit *www.facthound.com*
2. Choose your grade level.
3. Type in this book ID **0736864849** for age-appropriate sites. You may also browse subjects by clicking on letters, or by clicking on pictures and words.
4. Click on the **Fetch It** button.

FactHound will fetch the best sites for you!

READ MORE

Blashfield, Jean F. *The California Gold Rush.* We the People. Minneapolis: Compass Point Books, 2001.

Doeden, Matt. *John Sutter and the California Gold Rush.* Graphic Library. Mankato, Minn.: Capstone Press, 2006.

Ford, Carin T. *Levi Strauss: The Man Behind Blue Jeans.* Famous Inventors. Berkley Heights, N.J.: Enslow, 2004.

Peterson, Tiffany. *Levi Strauss.* Lives and Times. Chicago: Heineman Library, 2003.

Raatma, Lucia. *Levi Strauss.* Early Biographies. Minneapolis: Compass Point Books, 2004.

BIBLIOGRAPHY

Cray, Ed. *Levi's.* Boston: Houghton Mifflin, 1978.

Downey, Lynn. "Invention of Levi's 501 Jeans." Levi Strauss & Co. http://www.levistrauss.com/about/history/jeans.htm

INDEX

Battery Street store, 18–19
Bavaria, Germany, 7, 28

California, 4, 7, 8, 10, 11
    Gold Rush, 4–5, 6
    routes to, 5, 8, 9
    San Francisco, 4, 10, 12,
        13, 18, 20, 24, 25, 28

Davis, Jacob, 20–21, 24, 25

Fremont and Market Street
    factories, 24

jeans, 24, 25, 26, 27, 28, 29
    Levi's 501, 25, 27

Kentucky, 6, 8

legends, 12, 16, 28
Levi Strauss & Company,
    19, 20, 27, 28

materials for pants
    canvas, 13, 14, 15, 16, 17
    denim, 17, 20, 24, 26,
        28, 29
    duck, 29
miners, 12, 14, 15, 16, 28
mining camps, 15

New York City, 8, 28

Panama, 5, 8, 9
patent, 21, 22

Stern, David (brother-in-law),
    13, 14, 18
Stern, Fanny (sister), 13, 14,
    16, 19, 22, 28
Strauss, Jonas (brother),
    8, 17, 28
Strauss, Levi
    as a bachelor, 22, 25
    birth of, 28
    death of, 28
    name of, 28
    parents of, 7, 8, 28
    as a peddler, 6–7
Strauss, Louis (brother),
    8, 17, 28

trademarks
    back pocket design, 22,
        23, 27
    leather patch, 25, 27
    red tab, 27
    rivets, 20, 21, 22, 23,
        28, 29

waist-high overalls, 17, 19,
    21, 22, 23, 25, 26